DON'T THEY
MAKE A LOVELY
COUPLE?

Hey Akka,
You guys sure
make a lovely couple !!.
love you loads.
Diana

You guys are one
amazing pair of smileys! :)
Pray that you'll keep smiling
with God by your side all
your life!

All the best,
Akka.

Congrats Ann & paul

DON'T THEY MAKE A LOVELY COUPLE?

Six Important Questions
You Need To Face
About Your Marriage

By John and Ann Benton

*I love you
aleka,

R. Ann
R. shekina*

CHRISTIAN FOCUS

ISBN 1-84550-046-6

© Copyright John & Ann Benton 2005

10 9 8 7 6 5 4 3 2 1

Published in 2005
by
Christian Focus Publications, Ltd
Geanies House, Fearn, Tain,
Ross-shire, IV20 1TW, Great Britain.

www.christianfocus.com

Cover Design by Alister MacInnes

Printed and bound by
Nørhaven Paperback A/S, Denmark

Contents

This book is dedicated to

Adrian and Sarah
Arthur and Eileen
Klaus and Suzanne
Phil and Monika

with love and appreciation for your godly
priorities and example to God's people at
Chertsey Street.

Preface

We had to run away together in order to write this book. Life is very busy! (Many thanks must go to David and Judith Fuhr for allowing us to use their excellent bolt-hole on the South Coast).

As we separately wrote our pre-allocated chapters and then read each other's work, an interesting, though perhaps unsurprising, feature emerged: each of us was writing in his/her own voice. In effect, one of the points we make in this book was being demonstrated. The discerning reader will spot the distinction in style: in three chapters the male direct approach; analytical and logical; in three chapters the female country road: intuitive and personal. No attempt has been made to unify the voices into a corporate house style. Rather, it is to be hoped that, as is intended in marriage, the male and female contributions complement each other effectively.

John & Ann Benton

Introduction

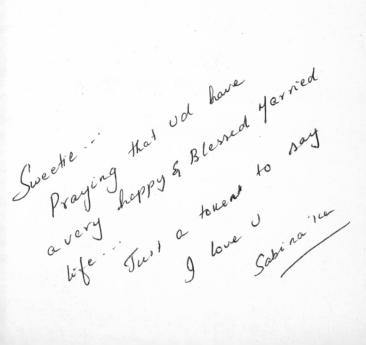

Sweetie... Praying that u'd have a very happy & Blessed Married life... Just a token to say I love u

Sabina 'ce

Welcome

Depend On

Honour

J ESUS

for successful life

now & in future

With love

Shendh.

15 July 2006.

We got married in September 1970. It was a blazing hot day: the men sweated in their top hats and tails and we all squinted at the camera.

The preparations for our wedding day, (although modest by today's standards) had been substantial and had largely been made by our parents: all we had to do was turn up. By contrast the preparations for our marriage meanwhile had been, in any explicit sense, non-existent, but implicitly they too were made by our parents. They were the generation that sang 'Love and marriage, love and marriage, go together like a horse and carriage.' They believed in marriage and believed it was, ''til death do us part', a safe, solid and sensible context for raising children and for life itself, even if they did not know why. We benefited from the security generated by that philosophy.

But we ourselves were the generation that sang 'All you need is love, dum da dada da'. That same generation went on to prove the falsity of that statement by divorcing in unprecedented numbers. Divorce rates continued to rise throughout the remainder of the twentieth century. Cohabitation is now the preferred option of many twenty-first century couples, anxious not to repeat their parents' mistakes. Not that there is any guarantee of permanence there.

The result of all this is, among many other tragedies, utter confusion about what marriage is. What should a couple expect of marriage? Why does it go wrong? What can be done to prevent it going sad and stale?

This book is written to answer such questions. Lovely couples too frequently end up at loggerheads. They need more than love: they need truth. We all do. Truth is to be found first and foremost in the Bible, the Maker's instructions. Apparently, only 1 in 10 people refer to the user guide of any newly purchased gadget for the home – until the thing breaks down, that is. Probably rather less than 1 in 10 look at what the Bible has to say about marriage before entering the married state. But God's truth is for everyone and wherever it is acted upon, it does good.

By the grace of God and the application of his truth, the knot so carelessly tied 33 years and 6 months ago has held, to the increasing, if not uninterrupted, delight of ourselves and our family. The grace and truth continue to be a daily necessity, however, and so it is with a due sense of humility and thankfulness, that we pass on what we have learned of God's truth concerning marriage, to others.

Chapter 1

What?

Be a Model
for the rest of
us to follow.

— Yours Ever.

Stevens.

[Thumbi Paapa]....!

We live in a very secular society. Our tendency is to explain everything in human terms. Marriage is thought of as an institution dreamed up centuries ago by our ancestors, which may have been appropriate back then, but may not be so helpful now. Times have changed. What may have suited Fred and Wilma Flintstone as they eked out an existence in their pre-historic cave need not necessarily be best for us living in the twenty-first century. We need to experiment with other possibilities in human relationships and explore other definitions of 'family.' That is the way many of our contemporaries think.

However, when we consider the question about what marriage is, the first thing we need to take on board is that it is not a merely human construction. Marriage is actually God's idea. The Bible tells us that having initiated the human race by creating Adam, it was God who said, *It is not good for the man to be alone* (Genesis 2:18) and then proceeded, to Adam's delight, to make Eve and sponsor the first marriage.

Marriage is therefore a divine gift to humanity. There is a wisdom about it which transcends different cultures and historical periods. It is not a hit or miss, 'give it a try', piece of kit. It may not be plain sailing, but handled rightly it is something we can have confidence in because it comes from our loving Creator. When we commit ourselves to marriage, we are committing ourselves to something we were designed for.

AN ALL-ROUND WINNER

Here are two observations which point to the divine origin of marriage.

First, marriage is not something we wayward human beings find easy. Naturally men and women find it difficult to rise to the standards set by God's wisdom – hence the rejection of marriage by many people today. Men especially, struggle to be faithful to one partner. Fidelity does not come naturally. Therefore, marriage really does not look like an idea which was just a line of least resistance, accidentally hit upon by our forebears. Casual sex may bring some kind of immediate gratification, but marriage is something quite difficult. Nevertheless, historically you find some form of marriage enshrined as the cornerstone of society across all the major cultures of the world. It does not appear to be something we would dream up for ourselves. It comes from God.

This brings us to the second pointer to the fact that marriage emerged from the wisdom of our Maker. Young people, especially in the

Western world, have experimented with different kinds of relationships between the sexes over the last half century. This has attracted a lot of attention from the social scientists, many of whom have a secular-liberal outlook on life and are not, at least initially, pro-marriage. Nevertheless, research has shown repeatedly that generally speaking, marriage, especially in the long term, is an all round winner for all parties. It is good for men; it is good for women; it is good for children. (We will look in more detail at some of these findings in a later chapter). When marriage is field tested it beats all other competitors. That is what you would expect of a relationship which is God's idea.

Once we understand this we can approach the adventure of marriage very positively.

When Adam met Eve

Having said that being solitary was not what he had in mind for Adam, God then contradicted the old proverb that a dog is a man's best friend. He proved to Adam that mere animals, interesting as they are in many ways, would not fulfil his need for a close companion.

> Now the Lord God had formed out of the ground all the beasts of the field and all the birds of the air. He brought them to the man to see what he would name

them; and whatever the man called each living creature, that was its name. So the man gave names to all the livestock, the birds of the air and all the beasts of the field. But for Adam no suitable helper was found (Genesis 2:19-20).

'Do I want to spend the rest of my life with this chimpanzee?' 'What would it be like sharing my bathroom with a water buffalo?' Adam concluded against.

So this is how Scripture describes God's next move.

So the LORD God caused the man to fall into a deep sleep; and while he was sleeping, he took one of the man's ribs and closed up the place with flesh. Then the LORD God made a woman from the rib he had taken out of the man, and he brought her to the man (Genesis 2:21, 22).

God performed surgery on Adam. He fashioned Eve from part of Adam and then presented her to him. Next we are told of Adam's reaction.

The man said, 'This is now bone of my bones and flesh of my flesh; she shall be called woman, for she was taken out of man' (Genesis 2:23).

The fact that Adam was elated at seeing Eve is plain as we recognise that these words, in the original language of the Old Testament, are the first human poetry recorded in the Bible. He is so deeply delighted, fascinated and moved by the sight of his woman that, like many a young guy in following generations, he composes a song. The word of God then goes on to draw a conclusion about marriage.

> For this reason a man will leave his father and mother and be united to his wife, and they will become one flesh (Genesis 2:24).

Marriage comes from God and takes place because God made man and woman specifically to be together. The genders are not from different planets! Woman has emerged from the very same body as the man. It is natural for them to be together – to be one. 'Do I want to spend the rest of my life with her? Yes, please!'

So What is Marriage?

Marriage is a big commitment. When people contemplate marriage they might hesitate and think to themselves, 'What am I getting into here?' That is a sensible and understandable question to ask. So we need to know what marriage is.

From what we have seen from Genesis we can draw up a simple definition of marriage. It would be something like this: 'Marriage is an exclusive covenant oneness between a man and a woman in the presence of God.'

Let me unpack that a little. As we think about what we have read in Genesis we realise that a number of things are going on.

First, it all takes place in the presence of the Lord. It was the Lord, who anaesthetised Adam initially, took the rib and fashioned Eve. It was God who presented Eve to Adam. It was to God that Adam addressed his poem concerning his girl.

Second, the marriage relationship is exclusive to one man and one women. That was God's design from the beginning and this is the pattern we must keep. When Princess Diana said in that famous interview with Martin Bashier, 'There were three of us in this marriage,' she was referring to Prince Charles' relationship to Camilla Parker-Bowles and she was saying that it was not right. In the Bible, where people like Abraham or Jacob got involved in polygamy it always led to trouble (Genesis 21:10; 30:1).

Third, it is a relationship between a man and a woman. God did not make Adam and Steve, nor did he make Madam and Eve. It is good to have close friends of the same sex. But marriage is to be across the genders. After all, one of God's purposes in giving marriage was that children might be born (Genesis 1:28).

Fourth, there is a covenant being made here. The word 'covenant' is a legal term. Dictionaries define it as 'a formal sealed agreement.' What Adam says about Eve in his poem is not simply a description of where she has come from. It is a declaration, in the presence of God, of what she is and what he wants her to be. He does not speak in the past tense saying, 'She was bone of my bone....' Rather he speaks in the present tense, *She is now bone of my bone and flesh of my flesh.* The use of the word *now* emphasises that Adam is speaking about the present not the past. His happy declaration of intent to be one with her takes place before God, the universal judge, and constitutes a formal legal agreement. Marriage is a covenantal relationship and is referred to as such throughout the Bible (see for example Malachi 2:14). This formal, covenantal side of marriage may seem not so relevant to the contemporary mindset which champions spontaneity and informality. However, it is there for many good reasons.

- Making a covenant before God encourages our partners to enjoy the fact that we are serious about wanting our relationship to work. It engenders confidence.
- Making a binding agreement before God is meant as a protection. We are answerable to God for how we treat our marriage partners.
- Making a covenant of marriage in God's presence is a public declaration of the beginning of a new family. It invites society at large to respect this relationship.
- Making such a covenant also displays something of the dignity of who we are as human beings. It lends nobility to us, and shows respect for our partner. We are not just animals moved by instinct. We are those, who before God, reflect on what we are doing and what it means to be committed to each other, and make choices we take seriously.

But fifthly, of course, something else is happening in this meeting of Adam and Eve. This covenant and all the other matters we have mentioned simply form the framework in which the heart of marriage is worked out. The essence of the marriage is the oneness between the husband and his wife, between the wife and her husband.

THE HEART OF MARRIAGE

> For this reason a man will leave his father
> and mother and be united to his wife, and
> they will become one flesh (Genesis 2:24).

The man and his wife become *united*. They
become a team. Though they are separate
individuals with different personalities and
qualities and talents, from now on, they are
on the same side. They face the game of life
together.

This unity means that wife and husband
will need to understand each other and agree
together. Though they may have different
responsibilities within the marriage, they
will have the same values, the same overall
attitudes, the same goals in life. This oneness
is not the purpose of marriage. It is a mistake
to think it is. Such thinking turns a marriage in
on itself and makes a marriage rather cloying
and narrow. We will take up the aim of marriage
later in the book. But, though oneness is not
the purpose of marriage, it is the essence of a
marriage. It is the *sine qua non* of a marriage.
It is the engine without which the car doesn't
go anywhere.

The sexual relationship, the man and the
woman becoming *one flesh*, is the physical
expression of being one with each other at

heart. Perhaps you can think of a human being as being composed of five parts. We are body, mind, emotions, will and spirit. (The spirit is what I call the 'true you.') Marriage partners are meant to have a oneness in all five of those areas.

- We are to be one in mind. That does not mean that we always think the same way. But it does mean that we must be able to agree together on all the important matters. We must have the same outlook on life. We must agree about how we raise children, how we use money, what we want out of life etc.

- We are to have an emotional oneness. Couples who cannot share their feelings are in for a pretty barren time. We need to be able to sympathise and feel for each other, especially as we face the inevitable problems which life throws at us.

- We must have a volitional unity. We need to have a oneness in what we will and choose in the big matters of life. If he chooses one place for a holiday while she chooses to go somewhere completely different, we are not looking at much of a relationship.

- We need to have a spiritual unity. We need to enjoy each other as we are. We need to be able to reveal 'the true me' knowing that we will be accepted and loved by our partner for the person we are.

This is what 'oneness' means in practice. It is about being agreed and intimate with each other across all these facets of our humanity. It means knowing each other, enjoying each other, and wanting the best for each other in our relationship. The sexual union of man and wife should be both a sign and an expression of oneness across these different areas of our personalities. Sexual intimacy is meant to be an outward, physical celebration of this inward intimacy and unity.

GETTING INTIMATE

If your oneness is not to be based on a lie, therefore, you have to be know one another. Intimacy is just a word which means knowing one another.

The Bible has three pictures of intimacy.

Nakedness. Commenting on Adam and Eve, the Bible says, *The man and his wife were both naked, and they felt no shame* (Genesis 2:25). They were open to each other. There was no cover up. Nothing was veiled. There were no masks.

Sexual intercourse. Later Genesis goes on to speak about sexual intercourse between Adam and Eve. My version of the Bible says, *Adam lay with his wife Eve, and she became pregnant and gave birth to Cain* (Genesis 4:1). But the original language of the Old Testament just says that Adam knew his wife Eve. It is the word just used for knowing things, like Noah knowing that the waters of the flood had receded (Genesis 8:11). By its use of the ordinary word *know* in this way, the Bible indicates that sexual intercourse is itself a picture of intimacy. There is a penetration and reception. There is an entering into the inner world of the other person and allowing the other person to enter your inner world and know you. When you are truly intimate with someone you know them on the inside and they know you similarly.

Face to face. A final picture of intimacy is the Bible's use of the phrase *face to face*. God spoke to many prophets in the Old Testament. But often he did so in obscure ways which were not easy to understand. But the Bible tells us that Moses he spoke *face to face, clearly and not in riddles* (Numbers 12:8). Sometimes we can misunderstand people on the telephone because we cannot see their face. 'Were those words meant to be ironic? Or was she being honest?' If only we could have seen the expression on her face it would have been clearer to us. That *face to face* confrontation that is sometimes necessary between people, is about honesty and getting to the truth. This is another picture of the knowing and being known which is what intimacy is all about.

Obviously intimacy is something that has to be worked at. Communication is essential to understanding one another. But some people just do not find it easy to express themselves. Then there are risks involved. When you open up to somebody you make yourself vulnerable. 'What will they do if they know what I am really like?'

We have seen that marriage is the exclusive covenant oneness between a man and a woman in the presence of God. The two become one. Intimacy therefore, is at the heart of marriage. But building intimacy takes time and effort and taking risks. We might wonder therefore whether it is worth it. There are two incalculable benefits of building an intimate marriage.

An intimate marriage is a strong marriage. Where ties are deep they are not easily broken. Think of a hurricane force wind blowing across the landscape. Trees with shallow roots will be torn up by the wind and fall. But where a tree's roots go deep into the land, it makes it strong. The wind cannot wrench it out of the ground.

It has strength to withstand the storm. The depth of intimacy in marriage is like the depth of a tree's roots. It gives us strength to stand. There are many hurricanes we have to face. At present there is a terrific hurricane of sexual immorality and temptation blowing across the Western world. Many marriages are not strong enough and get blown away. Sexual temptation is not the only storm your marriage may face. Perhaps there will be a storm of serious illness, financial disaster or disappointment in business which would seek to tear you apart. But where marriages have a deep intimacy there is much more likelihood that they will survive and come through in good shape.

The Bible puts it in very practical terms. *Two are better than one, because they have a good return for their work: If one falls down, his friend can help him up. But pity the man who falls and has no-one to help him up! Also, if two lie down together, they will keep warm. But how can one keep warm alone? Though one may be overpowered, two can defend themselves* (Ecclesiastes 4:9-12).

An intimate marriage is an enjoyable marriage. Remember what God said about Adam at the beginning; *It is not good for the man to be alone* (Genesis 2:18). God said that about Adam while he was in paradise, in the unspoiled Garden of Eden. At this time, before the Fall of mankind into sin, there were no storms, no troubles. Yet life was not as good as it could have been for Adam. Human beings find joy and happiness as they find friendship, companionship and intimacy. God's provision for Adam and Eve was each other. Through an intimate marriage we have a great opportunity for joy beyond anything we have known before.

Marriage is a covenant of oneness. It is worth working at. It will need working at.

Chapter 2

Who?

David Beckham says in his autobiography: 'My wife picked me out of a football sticker book. And I chose her off the telly.'

Is that really how it is done? Do we walk around the supermarket of life and pick off the shelf the one we want to be with, rather as we might pick a meal from the chill-food cabinet in Marks and Spencer? 'Whom will I marry?' is the stuff of adolescent day-dreams, but it is also a worthwhile question.

Some people may be surprised to discover that the Bible sets some specific limits on your choice. We will look at that under the first section: limitation.

The Bible can also tell you a great deal about your marriage partner in advance of your choice. This is fortune-telling beyond the 'you will meet a tall, dark handsome stranger' type. This is truth about human beings, which it is advisable to bear in mind before you commit to spend the rest of your life with one of the species. That will form the second section: expectation.

Thirdly, there is the question of Miss or Mr Right. You may have played an ice-breaker game at a party where everyone has a name from a famous partnership pinned to his or her back and the aim is, by asking roundabout questions of each other, to discover your own identity and link yourself up correctly the appropriate partner. There is only one for you. Is that how it is with marriage? The third section is sub-titled: destination.

A. LIMITATION

I. *You marry someone of the opposite sex*
That reduces the choice by half at a stroke! Did I hear someone laugh? Most people would say that they would no sooner think of marrying someone of the same gender as themselves than they would of marrying their own granny. It is, quite instinctively, an appalling idea. But few are prepared to acknowledge that this restriction is not merely one we might impose on ourselves out of personal taste; it is a restriction which is imposed by God from the beginning. And, like everything else in creation, it is good.

It is also purposeful.

> The LORD God said, 'It is not good for the man to be alone. I will make a helper suitable for him' (Genesis 2:18).

Woman was made differently from Adam: he was made from the ground which would be the focus of his work; she was made from him and her focus would be him. He was to take care of the garden; she was to be his helper and there was, and is, nothing derogatory or demeaning about that, for God himself is described as a helper (e.g., Exodus 18:4; Psalm 46:1).

Male and female were created equally to bear God's image and rule over creation (Genesis 1:27, 28) but they were created deliberately different to fulfil different functions and to complement each other.

The famous comment by Matthew Henry on Genesis 2:21-24 always bears repeating. He wrote that the woman was 'not made out of his (i.e. the man's) head to top him, not out of his feet to be trampled upon by him, but out of his side to be equal with him, under his arm to be protected, and near to his heart to be beloved.'

There is absolutely no Scriptural case for same-sex marriages. They are not a viable alternative; they are a sinful aberration and the very fact that the idea is gaining acceptance and popularity is itself a token of God's judgement on our society and nation (see Romans 1) and therefore a serious matter indeed.

To those for whom this truth, that marriage is a mixed gender affair, is not a problem, it is generally a great joy. Hooray for heterosexuality! *Vive la difference!*

However, the difference, as much as it can be enjoyed, is also a source of tension. This is one of the cosmic results of the rebellion of Adam and Eve to God's ways back in that garden of Genesis 3. Eve was told that the husband/wife relationship would be soured because she would have an inordinate desire to control Adam instead of helping him.

But the creation pattern stands and remains the model for a good marriage. In this pattern the man is the principal provider and protector; he provides loving leadership for his wife. The woman is his helper. Her strongest muscles are not in her arms but in her womb to nurture life. The different design is seen not just in anatomy but in physiology and neurology. The male brain is wired to focus on one task at a time and see it through; the female brain is wired, as a mother's has to be, to multi-task. Male hormones produce an aggressive drive and the willingness to take risks; female hormones produce sensitivity and intuition. Both have their part to play in the task of survival in the world. Put them together in a marriage and you have a formidable team.

2. *You marry a Christian (assuming you are one yourself)*

So you are looking for someone of the opposite sex; there are still plenty of fish in the sea or even dogs off the lead! But remember this –

they are not all going in the same direction and that could turn out to be crucial.

A believer must marry a fellow believer. God says so.

> Do not be yoked together with unbelievers. For what do righteousness and wickedness have in common? Or what fellowship can light have with darkness? What harmony is there between Christ and Belial? What does a believer have in common with an unbeliever? (2 Corinthians 6:14, 15; [see also I Corinthians 7:39]).

If you are a believer in the Lord Jesus Christ, then God's Spirit lives in you. Now marriage is the most intimate human relationship there is; God's Holy Spirit cannot comfortably co-exist with an anti-Christian attitude, otherwise known as idolatry. And there is no in-between. Nor is there room for some kind of mitigating plea of aiming to bring the unbelieving partner to faith, even though you may be able to quote cases where this has happened. God is always much kinder than we deserve. And there are many instances one could cite where the influence has gone in the other direction. What God does ask of us is obedience. In return we have the promise that he honours those who honour him (I Samuel 2:30) and that those who delight themselves in God (first and foremost) will be given the desires of their heart (Psalm 37:4).

A little thought will enable you to see also the practical sense of this command. An unequal yoke might be manageable for a short time but is ultimately very uncomfortable and a cause of great pain; so is a marriage between a Christian and a non-Christian. You want a harmonious marriage but if you are a believer and your partner is not, you are not, to borrow the cliché, singing from the same song-sheet. Even if you went to the same school, support the same football team and both enjoy eighties glam-rock music (or something!) but one of you has been rescued by Jesus from the deserved condemnation for your sins and the other one is still drowning, what you have in common is minimal and trivial. Don't do it; don't go there; it is not a good idea.

(This is not to say that when two non-Christians marry and later in the marriage one of them becomes a Christian that there must be a divorce. If, in God's providence, someone in an existing marriage becomes a Christian while their partner does not, God is able to give special grace. See I Corinthians 7 for what Paul has to say on this kind of situation.)

B. Expectation

In the early part of the nineteenth century, Jane Austen observed in her novel, *Mansfield Park*, that 'there is not one in a hundred of either sex, who is not taken in when they marry ... it is, of all transactions, the one in which people expect most from others, and are least honest themselves.' Marriage can indeed be full of surprises and not all of them pleasant. That is why it is important to bear in mind the following two points:

1. *You marry a sinner*

You would not marry a sinner by choice, but there is no option. It might be cruel to point this out to someone in the first flush of romance, but your beloved is a sinner like you (Romans 3:10).

When you first form a friendship which has marriage potential, you are bound to see much which is delightful to you. First of all it might be the sparking blue eyes, the hilarious repartee, the stylish dress-sense; then as the acquaintance develops it might be the tender sensitivity to the needs of others, the disciplined attitude to time, the generosity with money. You will see these points, or others like them, as utter positives. And of course they are certainly strengths. But the sinful nature in all of us will over-egg the pudding of our strong points, so that in the end, or from time to time, they are more like weak ones.

If you are in love, it will take you some time to discover this because the perception of your loved one is tinged with the rosy glow and hazy edges of your excitement over finding someone who pleases you so much, and who likes you to boot. That phase is described by some people as *idealisation*. It is followed in due course, perhaps within days of returning from the honeymoon, by *realisation*. This is about as welcome as a telephone call from someone trying to sell you a kitchen and much more difficult to deal with.

That stylish dress-sense you so much admired is less attractive when you discover a) that IKEA doesn't sell a wardrobe big enough for her clothes and shoes and b) that she has thrown out your favourite old sweater. That disciplined attitude to time, which so impressed you in courtship might mean that he cannot spend an afternoon just being with you without looking at his watch and telling you all the things he has to get done today. Love takes on a new dimension when the one you love does things which irritate you. No wonder the model of husbandly love is Christ and the church. Just think what Christ has to put up with from the church! And it comes as no surprise to him. He knew what we were when he took us on. Yet he gave himself for the church (Ephesians 5:25).

In a marriage there are two sinners, so let it come as no surprise that there will be difficulties, tensions and conflicts amidst the joy, excitement and togetherness.

2. *You marry someone with baggage*

It is not just your shoes, your CD collection and your old teddy bear that you will bring with you when you start your married life. It is all those significant experiences which have shaped your life and opinions. Even little things tell: perhaps you thought there was only one way to make gravy or clean a toilet until you saw your partner do it. Presumably there is plenty of room for compromise on such points. Perhaps you grew up on different continents or in contrasting cultures. Such things will have shaped your expectations about marriage and you probably need more time to get to know and understand each other. This is one kind of baggage.

Another kind is the sum of our experiences, possibly extremely serious and telling: a bereavement or a divorce in the family, abuse, failures, illnesses, disappointments. These are things which can affect us and our personality. These are things which drive us to make resolutions which include the word 'never', convictions which we cling to as a protective strategy against further pain.

All baggage needs unpacking, together with your partner in the interest of mutual understanding. It also needs to be brought to the light of Scripture. Not everything we learn from our families and upbringing is true and right. We live in a climate where we are encouraged to blame others for the way we think and act and are. We think it is enough to say, 'it is because such and such happened when I was a child', and thus leave sinful attitudes and behaviours unchallenged. But God's word does challenge us and holds each of us responsible for our own behaviour and responses, even to traumatic events beyond our control (Ezekiel 18:20). We need to examine and chuck out our own sinful baggage along with our Rolf Harris records. Then perhaps we can encourage our partners to do the same.

C. DESTINATION

1. *You marry your best friend*
Some Christians get very hung up about finding the 'right one'. They worry lest their lives should

turn out like a Thomas Hardy novel, where the protagonists are always omitting to read the crucial letter or turning up at the wrong address. Thomas Hardy had no understanding of the God of the Bible and subscribed to a bitter and fatalistic worldview. Such a worldview is enough to drive anyone crackers. But the Bible presents us with a sovereign God who works all things out for those who love him for their ultimate good (Romans 8:28). Surely this is what keeps us sane: we have a great and good God. It is beyond our understanding how God both directs our feet and our choices and yet holds us responsible for them, but both things are true. Why should everything that Almighty God does be comprehensible to our feeble brains? He is not answerable to us but we are to him. And what he asks of us is that we should obey his commands and trust him by walking in his ways and seeking first his kingdom and his righteousness (Matthew 6:33).

The apostle Paul reminds us that it is absolutely fine and excellent to be single (I Corinthians 7:8), particularly for the sake of the gospel work. But marriage is the right and good course for those who recognise that it is not good for them to be alone (I Corinthians 7:9). They need that companionship and intimacy which only comes through marriage.

Such a Christian will prayerfully pursue the acquaintance of Christians of the opposite sex and trust the Lord that where a friendship deepens it may develop into something more which is pleasing to both parties. There does not have to be a name written in the sky. But if all other things are in place, i.e. you are both seeking to walk with God and glorify him, then it would seem to be enough that you like each other. Go to it! There does have to be some chemistry: see the Song of Solomon for the kind of thing. God spoke of Ezekiel's wife as the 'delight of his eyes.' Malachi 2:14 refers to a wife as a partner; in Proverbs 5:19 she is described as a loving doe, a graceful deer. It all sounds like very good fun.

2. *You marry an agent of your sanctification*
It isn't just fun though. As a Christian you will be aware that your life is but a journey. You are on your way to a wedding, not your wedding to the bride or groom of your choice in this life, but the wedding of the Lamb (Revelation 19:7). This is the real marriage; that between Christ and the church at the end of the age, and you will be part of that bride on that great day.

So what is your life about? It is about getting ready for that occasion, just as a bride makes her preparations to be at her most beautiful on her wedding day. In one sense you could describe the whole of your life as marriage preparation. We are being shaped and beautified from the time of our first coming to Christ to the day we die. This is the work of sanctification, in which we are told to actively participate with the Holy Spirit (Galatians 5:16-25).

But how does it work in practice? Suppose God sees that you are very short on patience, what does he do? He gives you his word which tells you that you should clothe yourself with patience (Colossians 3:12) and then he sends you someone to test that patience, so that you find out your lack and humble yourself and cry to him for help. He answers that cry for help and you make progress but he tests you again and again, exposing your weakness and causing to lean more and more on him. So you learn and you change. You become more beautiful; you become more like Jesus.

Now very often the person he sends to you, to expose that weakness which needs attention, will be none other than your chosen partner in life, whom you love but who from time to time, because you are both sinners, drives you nuts. Meanwhile you are the same useful tool in God's hand in the life of your husband or wife. So while you are learning to live and love together you are also being shaped to be more like Christ, which is the main plot of the story of which your life and marriage is a sub-plot (Romans 8:29). I think that makes the adventure of marriage even more exciting than *The Lord of the Rings* and certainly more romantic than Mills and Boon.

Chapter 3

Why?

It is no secret that for the past two generations a smaller percentage of people in Britain have been getting married. At the same time there has been an increased incidence and acceptance of divorce, living together, pre-marital sex and having children out of wedlock.

There are many voices in modern society which ask, 'Why bother to get married?' To walk up the aisle is to go against the flow. It is to be out of step with many of our contemporaries. It is to swim against the tide. You might say, 'Give me three good reasons why we should want to get married?' That is exactly what I am going to do in this chapter. My reasons are pictorial, personal and practical.

I. The Pictorial Reason

Some people yawn and switch off at the very mention of the word 'theology'. But that is a great mistake. Theology is the study of God. The world in which we live is his world, and God himself is our ultimate environment. In him we live and move and have our being (Acts 17:28). The theologian Jim Packer has put the importance of understanding God and his ways like this:

'Knowing about God is crucially important for the living of our lives. As it would be cruel to an Amazonian tribesman, to fly him to London, to put him down without explanation in Trafalgar Square and leave him, as one who knew nothing of English or England, to fend for himself, so we are cruel to ourselves if we try to live in this world without knowing about the God whose world it is and who runs it. The world becomes a strange, mad, painful place, and life in it a disappointing and unpleasant business, for those who do not know about God. Disregard the study of God and you sentence yourself to stumble and blunder through life blindfold.'[1]

God had his own reason for making male and female and bringing them together in marriage. Human beings are made in God's image and the fundamental purpose which God had in making us was that we should be his representatives on earth to the rest of creation. God is invisible, but within the visible universe there should be a living picture of what the Creator is like. And that picture is us – human beings. We are here to point to the glory and wonder of God. Sadly, since mankind's Fall into sin, that picture has been very much marred and distorted, yet nevertheless it is still there (James 3:9).

1. *Knowing God*, by J I Packer, Hodder & Stoughton, p. 17.

As individuals we are created in God's image, and it should not surprise us to find that Scripture tells us that the primary human relationship of marriage, also has a God-glorifying pictorial purpose. This is how the apostle Paul puts it:

To the woman in a marriage he says:

> Now as the church submits to Christ, so also wives should submit to their husbands in everything (Ephesians 5:24).

To the man in a marriage he writes:

> Husbands, love your wives, just as Christ loved the church and gave himself up for her... (Ephesians 5:25).

Later he goes on to quote from Genesis and then again turn our attention to the fact that human marriage is a picture of something far deeper.

> 'For this reason a man will leave his father and mother and be united to his wife, and the two will become one flesh.' This is a profound mystery – but I am talking about Christ and the church (Ephesians 5:31, 32).

Human marriage is meant to be a graphic representation of the relationship between

Jesus and his people, and therefore of the love of God for us. The way Paul uses the text from Genesis 2:24, indicates that this was true from the very beginning. It was not that God was looking around for some illustration of how Christ loves the church and just happened to light upon marriage and think, 'Oh that would represent it nicely.' Rather it was the other way round. Right from the beginning, when God made Adam and Eve and brought them together, he modelled the way they related to each other on Christ and the church.

When we go away on holiday most of us take a camera of some kind with us. We snap away at all the wonderful sights – the view from the high mountain, the sunset over the sea, the kids with their ice-creams. The mountain and the sea and the kids are the original, and the photos just give a representation of what it was really like. Just so, Christ and the church is the original, and every human married is meant to be a snapshot of that eternal relationship. Marriage is meant to point beyond itself to something far more profound. It is meant to point to the eternal love between God and his people.

Once we understand this, we are standing on the bedrock foundation of why marriage is right and other kinds of relationships are wrong.

- Why isn't co-habiting acceptable? The answer is because such a relationship refuses a legally binding commitment. But that is not how Jesus relates to the church. He has bound himself, before God his Father, to be our Saviour. Co-habitation sets a kind of limit on commitment. But Jesus' commitment to his people is unlimited.
- Why isn't sleeping around with multiple partners acceptable? Why is adultery wrong? It is because such behaviour misrepresents Christ. Jesus is faithful to his bride the church. He is never unfaithful.
- Why isn't sex before marriage acceptable? Ultimately because it does not please God. The Lord Jesus came the first time to win his bride. He will come a second time to bring her to the wedding feast and marry her (Revelation 19:5-8). Christ delays the full pleasures of the consummation which the church will experience until after his return when he publicly receives his bride.
- Why isn't a homosexual relationship acceptable? Because it misrepresents the relationship between Christ and the church. Christ and the church are not the same. They are different. He is our Saviour. We are those he has rescued. He

is the second Person of the Trinity. We are God's creatures.

- Why does God hate divorce (Malachi 2:16)? Why although he allows that in some circumstances it is necessary to prevent further evil, does God always lament over it? It is because it is a misrepresentation. Jesus will never divorce his bride.

These things give a false picture of Christ and the church to the universe and make God angry. Equally though, we can see that a dead, loveless 'Christian' marriage dishonours God. We do not simply need to get married, we need to make our marriages work.

So there is the first reason which answers the question, 'why marriage?'

2. THE PERSONAL REASON

Marriage has the potential to make us truly fulfilled as individual human beings. This is the second reason why marriage is the right choice over other kinds of relationships.

Remember God's statement, *It is not good for the man to be alone* (Genesis 2:18)? Why was it not good? Adam lived in paradise. The Fall had not yet taken place. He had a wonderful relationship with God? What more could he possibly need? But God knew that he did need something else – indeed someone else.

This takes us back to the fact that human beings are made in the image of God. The Bible teaches us the wonderful and mysterious truth of the Trinity. Though there is one God, there are three Persons who make up the Godhead – the Father, the Son and the Holy Spirit (2 Corinthians 13:14; Matthew 28:19). These three are all the same in that they are all God, but they are different in that they can legitimately be described differently as the Father, the Son and the Holy Spirit. They exist in a perfect, eternal relationship of love. This is why the Bible tells us, 'God is love' (1 John 4:8). Before ever the world was made, love existed! It existed within God himself. Love has an eternal quality about it, which in its best moments, even the Fallen world recognises. That is why though music styles may change, the lyrics of so many songs are about love. That is why Hollywood 'feel good' movies are so often about love.

If human beings are fundamentally made in God's image, and if human beings are to find personal fulfilment, they need to find love with others like themselves. Just as in the Trinity there is God-to-God love, so we need human-to-human love. That is why it was *not good* for Adam to be a solitary soul. Now of course, that love can take many legitimate forms. Children are to love parents and vice versa. Friends should love each other. In another way, neighbours need to love each other. But, the highest and primary avenue of such love is found in the loving marriage of male and female. It is in such love that we find the greatest earthly fulfilment.

One of the film star, Jack Nicholson's recent romantic comedy movies entitled *As Good As It Gets* makes this point very well. It is really a visual tract denouncing the atomisation and individualism of modern society. The film begins in an apartment block in a typical American city. Nicholson plays a writer who insists on being alone and undisturbed. He is obsessive about keeping to a strict daily routine, including sitting in the same place and being served by the same waitress at the local restaurant every day. There are various people living in the block, all pursuing their lives with a ferocious concern for their privacy and their egos. But they are all unhappy people. It is only as they become aware of the tragedies in one another's lives that they begin to reach out to one another and build relationships. The highlight of the film comes when having paid for her sick child to have specialist care in order that she can be at work and serve him lunch, Nicholson's character falls in love with the waitress. It is like a revelation to him. He reflects in astonishment on how he feels. He says to himself about this woman he loves, 'You make her laugh and you've got a life!' The greatest compliment he can think of to pay her is that he says to her from his heart, 'You make me want to be a better man.' And receiving such a compliment, she is thrilled to her heart. The message of the film is clear. Isolation means unhappiness. Love brings joy.

There are many people who think that they can find the joy without getting into the commitments and responsibilities which go with life-long marriage. But it doesn't work like that. Yes, there may be the initial thrill of making a new relationship. However, when the relationship runs into trouble there is no commitment there to keep it going. The average duration of a co-habiting relationship in Britain is around two years. Relationships like this break up and people get hurt. The result of that is that people take steps not to get so involved again. They may pursue another relationship, but this time they will not allow themselves to get in so deep as the last time in case they get their heart broken again. So they hold back. But at the same time, holding back will mean less intimacy, and therefore less enjoyment and fulfilment in the relationship. And so it goes on. When the next relationship comes along they hold themselves back even more and so on. Non-commitment nurtures a pattern of diminishing returns. Many who have gone through life like this end up on their own, lonely and bitter.

So we see the second answer to the question, 'why marriage?'

However, what of those who are not against marriage but stay single? There are many such excellent single people. Some choose to remain unmarried because they are more free to serve the Lord and take on difficult and dangerous tasks for him without having a marriage partner or a family (I Corinthians 7:7, 36-38). These people are often worth their weight in gold to the church. They are spiritual diamonds. But I know of very few who find their singleness easy to cope with. Right from the beginning human beings were made for marriage, and in marriage and family we can find the greatest joys this world has to offer.

3. The Practical Reason

With the changes in Western society concerning marriage and the family over recent decades, a lively debate has been sparked, and much research has been produced by sociologists comparing traditional marriage with the outcomes of other kinds of relationships which people choose to pursue.

If we accept that what is taught in the Bible about marriage comes from God himself the overall findings of this research should not surprise us. God loves us and wants the best for us. Based on the statistical evidence there is a growing consensus that marriage is 'an important social good, associated with an impressively broad array of positive outcomes for children and adults alike.'[2] The information used here comes from CIVITAS, The Institute for the Study of Civil Society which is an independent social policy think tank. It has no political or religious affiliations.

Obviously statistics give a general picture. They cannot give a certain answer about particular situations. But statistics do give us probabilities as to how things will go if we choose a particular path. Let me just headline some of the findings that have come to light through research in the Western world.

Marriage is associated with better health and lower rates of injury, illness and disability for both men and women. The most careful research

2. *Does Marriage Matter?* Civitas 2003; ISBN 1-903 386-31 4

into the health effects of marriage has taken place in the US. The incidence of major diseases in married, cohabiting, divorced, widowed and never married individuals was compared for 9,333 people in the 50s age group. 'Without exception,' the authors reported, 'married persons have the lowest rates of morbidity for each of the diseases, impairments, functioning problems and disabilities.'

Married couples build more wealth on average than singles or cohabiting couples. The economic advantages of marriage arise from more than just access to two incomes. For example economies of scale come into play. Married couples seem to receive more gifts from parents and grandparents than do cohabiters. Strangely, also, research finds that married men tend to earn more than single men. Why? The causes are not completely clear, but married men tend to have greater motivation in their work, less likelihood of resigning, healthier and more stable routines (including sleep, diet and alcohol consumption) and therefore attract promotion. Husbands also benefit from both the work effort and emotional support they receive from a committed wife.

Married mothers have lower rates of depression than do lone or cohabiting mothers. Lone mothers are seven times as likely as married mothers to report trouble with their 'nerves.' This is true even after corrections have been made for such factors as poverty. In the National Child Development Study, divorced and never-married mothers aged 33 were 2.5 times more likely than married mothers to experience high levels of psychological distress.

Marriage increases the likelihood that parents have good relationships with their children. Even after taking other factors into account, lone mothers were still twice as likely as married mothers to report that their child's behaviour was upsetting them. In Britain, less than half of children in lone-mother families see their fathers once a week, and the percentage is even smaller where the father was never married to his child's mother. It needs to be realised that 20% to 30% of non-resident fathers have not seen their children in the last year. There is even growing evidence that remaining in an unhappy marriage might have less of a negative effect on father-child relationships than divorce. Married fathers spend more time with their children.

Much more could be said, including the well-known fact that on average children from in-tact marriages do much better at school. Here, then we see that for down to earth practical reasons marriage wins out. This is the third reason why we should forsake other arrangements and commit ourselves to marriage.

Marriage is special. It is a gift from God. It is a relationship of enormous significance as it pictures Christ and the church. It is a relationship which, when rightly handled, has the potential to bring deep personal fulfilment in our lives. But not only so, sociologists are finding hard evidence that far from being out of date, marriage is still the best way for men and women to pursue a relationship.

Chapter 4

How?

We have learned that marriage is a covenant. Having made it in the presence of witnesses, can one not return the suit to the hirers, cover the dress in polythene and hang it in the wardrobe, and get on with life at a respectable distance, side by side?

Not if you want a strong marriage, not if you want a marriage that glorifies God, not if you want a mirror of Christ and the church. Do not underestimate the power of selfish sinful nature to freeze and to wreck the best of relationships. A strong marriage, like a well-kept house, needs a continuous rolling programme of attention and maintenance.

The Victorian author, George Eliot, observed this about married people in her book *Daniel Deronda*. 'In general mortals have a great power of being astonished at the presence of an effect towards which they have done everything, and at the absence of an effect towards which they have done nothing but desire it. Husbands and wives are mutually astonished at the loss of affection which they have taken no pains to keep.'

The point is, you have to do more than desire it. Unattended affection can and frequently does wither and die.

This chapter will suggest nine ways in which a strong marriage is built and maintained.

These nine ways can be arranged into an acrostic which spells TAKE RISKS. Of course, this is not to say that we recommended taking *risks* with your marriage. But you might be required to take a risk within your marriage, for example, by being truly open and honest, or by facing issues rather than hoping they will go away, or by being the first to say sorry even if it makes you look foolish. This is living dangerously but unlike extreme ironing, it has a serious purpose.

Self denial and sacrifice are crucial to a good marriage. They represent the way of Christ (Mark 8:34, 35) and so one would expect to see evidence of them in a Christian marriage.

I. TRUTHFULNESS
I have sometimes heard a wife say, 'I just don't know him anymore', or a husband say of his wife, 'It's like living with a stranger.'

This happens where a couple have neglected truthfulness. Truthfulness means more than not telling outright lies, although, of course, it includes that. Lying is non-communication and it rots relationships. But truthfulness means more. It means, to start with, identifying your own feelings or observations or experiences of day-to-day life to yourself, so that you can share them with your wife or husband. It means seeking to improve your ways of communicating such things.

So here you both are, meeting up after work:

'How was your day?'
'Fine. Yours?'
'OK.'

Is there really nothing more to say, no essential event, office joke, even trivial occurrence which you could share so that you could be part of each other's worlds? Your worlds of work may be vastly different or steeped in technical jargon, but there must be something, in the interest of truthfulness which you could offer as a window into the significant quantity of time you spend apart from each other.

Here is another situation which is against the spirit of truthfulness: making decisions which affect the whole family without including the other in the early stages of that decision.

'I've signed up for Marigold to have trumpet lessons.'
'I've booked for us to go on an extreme ironing adventure holiday.'
'I've replaced the lawn with purple decking.'

'I've bought an Irish Wolfhound puppy. He's called Nigel.'

A third typical anti-truthfulness scenario will be all too familiar, I fear.

'What's the matter?'
'Nothing.'
'Yes there is. I can tell.'
'It's nothing.'
'Have I done something wrong?'
'No.'

But of course there is something wrong. The one who replies 'nothing' is not only lying. He or she is engaging in a dangerous manipulative game, using silence as a weapon to make the other feel bad. The truth will probably be that there is something but it is so small that the wounded party is ashamed to spell it out lest it shrink to invisibility and then he or she will have no excuse for such bad behaviour. Ah, the sinful games that people play! Take the risk by answering the question, truthfully and lovingly (Ephesians 4:15).

2. APPRECIATION

There is a saying in teaching that 'there is no performance, however bad, that cannot be made worse by a lack of encouragement.'

People need to know that what they do is recognised and not taken for granted.

Have you noticed how repeatedly British people say 'thank you' to each other when they are shopping or ordering food in a restaurant? It is sometimes quite amusing to count.

It might be more enlightening to count how many times you have thanked or expressed appreciation to your partner in any given day. We tend to behave worst with the people we love best.

'How do I love thee? Let me count the ways,' wrote Robert Browning.

'Good game! Good game! Hope you're playing it at home!' quipped Bruce Forsyth.

Put these two interesting ideas together and you have a salutary activity for any married person: take pen and paper and list all the things you appreciate about your husband/wife and the things he or she does for you. Then look for an opportunity to share it.

'I love the way you painted the decking purple!'

The American author and humourist Mark Twain used to say, 'I can live for two months on a good compliment.' Can't we all! (Ephesians 4:29).

There are other ways of expressing appreciation apart from pretty speeches. You can say it with flowers, as Interflora will remind you, or with an e-mail or text, or with a smile or a treat, or by just spending time (see below). Go on. Take the risk.

3. Keep Short Accounts

It was not written exclusively for the context of marriage but the following words of the apostle Paul are particularly applicable to married people:

> Do not let the sun go down while you are still angry, and do not give the devil a foothold (Ephesians 4:26, 27).

Too many married people keep a record of wrongs and love to recite them, even years later.

> 'And another thing, you went and booked that ironing holiday without even consulting me!'
> 'That was in 1997!'

When two sinners live together, as we noticed earlier, the potential for grievous bodily and mental harm is enormous. The 1970 romantic weepie *Love Story* carried as its publicity slogan: *Love is never having to say you're sorry.* In the current vernacular: I don't think so! But how should we say sorry when we know we are in the wrong?

The Biblical model is the lost son of Luke 15:11-24. Notice in that story that there is an honest son owning up with no excuses. The son does not say to his father, 'I'm sorry ... but you shouldn't have given me the money.' No ifs, no buts, no blame-shifting, just taking responsibility for having messed up, and asking forgiveness.

> 'I was wrong. I should never have bought Marigold that trumpet without talking to you.'

These kind of speeches are unfamiliar in a therapeutic and litigious culture. But they are liberating life and breath to a marriage. It is worth taking the risk.

But granting forgiveness is not less difficult. By definition, forgiveness is never deserved. But Jesus says we must give it, again and again (Luke 17:1-10). And granting forgiveness is an act of the will, a decision made regardless of feelings. Did the servant who came in from the field *feel* like preparing his master's supper? No, it was just his duty. Here are some helpful steps in granting forgiveness:

a) Ask yourself, 'What actually was the sin?' – When you answer that question truly you may discover it is too trivial to mention, and this whole fracas has more to do with the fact that the next door neighbour's trumpet playing lost you some sleep last night.

b) If you need to take this further, start by remembering your own forgiveness (Matthew 18:21-35). How big was your debt which God wrote off?

c) On your knees before God, give up the right to be angry. This is the bit that hurts; this is taking up the cross.

d) Lovingly tell your partner the sin and in the same breath your forgiveness (Galatians 6:1-3).

e) Follow your words with some small but significant action which proves that the fault is mended and normal service is resumed. 'Let's take Nigel for a walk!'

To fail to do this seeking and granting forgiveness is deadly to a marriage. It is inviting the devil to be a permanent lodger in your home, where his chief delight down the years will be to nurture that root of bitterness until it destroys you and your marriage. By keeping short accounts and sorting matters out before bedtime, you show the devil the door and kick him firmly out.

4. EXPERIENCES

Life's experiences change us. Damien Rice, in his sad song *Cannonball* croons softly, but unfortunately truly, for many, 'Stones taught me to fly, love taught me to lie, life taught me to die, but it's not hard to fall when you float like a cannonball.'

So what shall we do with life's experiences? The world is full of dangers and disappointments. It also brings its occasional delights. Married people need to know that both losing and winning can shape their marriage and their lives for the good.

Together you build up a bank of memories, of shared joys when you celebrated and thanked God, or of poignant times when you wept and prayed together. Such times strengthen the bond.

But know also that triumphs and troubles can drive you apart.

Triumphs drive you apart when A is jealous of B's success. The first marriage of the actress Kate Winslett to a humble cameraman fell apart, so it was reported, for this kind of reason. Where there is no true sharing of the work and where two very separate lives are lived so that trust is eroded, this is likely to happen. Read again T for truthfulness.

Troubles drive you apart when you fail to realise that grief is expressed differently. It is a shocking fact that couples who suffer the loss of a child in a tragic early death all too frequently go on to lose each other in the death of their marriage. He thinks she blames him. She thinks he blames her. But nothing is said. The very helplessness of such a ghastly situation can make people put up the barriers in the interest of self- protection. Simply put, they do not trust each other enough to share their darkest thoughts, which would help them to deal with them. And trust cannot be created in the crisis; it must be pre-established.

The moving story of the brilliant mathematician, John Nash was told in the award-winning film *A Beautiful Mind*. While still a young man, John Nash suffered from huge and eventually alarming delusions and was diagnosed as schizophrenic. He could not tell truth from fantasy. His behaviour was so peculiar and disturbing it all but wrecked his marriage to Alicia. But in a moment of tenderness in the film, Alicia takes John's hand and puts it to her cheek and tells him, 'This is real.' Their facing of his illness together saves him and their marriage. How fitting that, years later, when John Nash is awarded the Nobel Prize for his contribution to Mathematics and Economics, in his acceptance speak he deliberately shares his moment of triumph with

Alicia, acknowledging that the mystery of love is beyond reason and the most powerful force in the universe. No Christian would disagree with that.

To build a strong marriage we have seen four things you must TAKE (Truthfulness; Appreciation; Keeping short accounts and using Experiences positively). Now for the RISKS.

5. ROMANCE

I do not just mean by romance, roses, chocolates and a walk on the decking in the moonlight. Those things are excellent and I am always delighted to see an older married couple walk hand in hand or give each other a look across a crowded room. Similarly it is a sad thing to see a couple who have let themselves go, who no longer think it is important to make an effort for each other, whether in dress, appearance, manners or speech.

The second most popular book in the English language, according to the BBC poll in 2003, was Jane Austen's *Pride and Prejudice*. It owes its popularity, I suspect, not merely to its fine characterisation and witty observations but to the sheer perfection of its romance. Not the smutty romance of boy meets girl, you'll do for me, let's go back to my place. This is high romance with a capital R. Darcy loves Elizabeth; he demonstrates it by resolutely and sacrificially going to a massive amount of trouble and expense to sort out the desperate mess which her family is in. He does this without her knowledge, when he thinks he has no hope of winning her. Then she finds out and thanks him and he replies in the most tingling of love speeches, that when he did it he was not thinking of her family, 'I believe I thought only of you.' Ah! No wonder half the population of Britain (the female half) fell in love with Colin Firth when he played the part of Mr Darcy in the BBC adaptation of the novel. This is the manliness we long for. It is also Biblical, Christ-like manliness to which every husband should aspire.

There is a lot of pompous stuff talked about headship and submission, which can make it sound unattractive and terrifying to both sexes. But headship means sacrificial service of the most beautiful type. And submission is the glad and cheerful response to a husband who is not Mr Darcy and most certainly not Christ, but who within the covenant of marriage is your God-given leader.

This is true romance. Loving, sacrificial leadership and respectful submission are foundational in a good and happy marriage.

And they will emerge to light up any given wet Saturday, where a man thinks of what would please his wife and a wife thinks of what would please her husband. And they act upon it! At the time it may seem like a risky strategy. But he who dares, wins!

6. INITIATION

You can't write a book about marriage and not talk about sex, so now is the time for shy British people to study a speck on the carpet, or to put a brown paper cover on this book.

Sex is God's idea, that is the first truth to grasp, and it is a central feature of marriage. It is intimacy acted out. It is rather sad that during the last century Christians appeared to put sex into the hands of pornographers and makers of programmes on Channel 4. Those people in their turn have not understood its importance and have portrayed it generally as an animal function, albeit an intriguing one. In doing so they have degraded and demoralised what was intended to be the supreme expression between a man and his wife of commitment and love. Sex has also been most truly described as a source of truth and consolation, but that is an aspect which will rarely be seen in a steamy soap-opera scene.

Good sex is not the prerogative of the young and so-called liberated. Recent research from the US suggested that, in fact, the most sexually fulfilled group are married people between the ages of 50 and 60.

There are too many lies or misconceptions told about sex which can ruin it for a couple before they start. Here, for example, are a few such lies:

- Good sex solves other problems in marriage.
- Proper sex must be serious and solemn.
- Unless you are making love, frequently, creatively and ecstatically, your sex-life is substandard.
- Unless the woman experiences an orgasm every time, something is wrong.
- Sex is a woman's duty and she must submit to it however degrading and painful it is to her.
- Sex is a clever tool in power plays to manipulate your partner into getting what you desire.

Lies such as these cause anxiety and misery; they also inhibit sexual expression. It is a bad idea to bring to the marriage bed ideas about right sexual behaviour which you have gleaned from colleagues, parents, Cosmopolitan magazine or the back of the bike-sheds at school.

The expression 'making love' is a good one, for it implies rightly that a couple create, probably over many years, their own private and unique sex-life which benefits both and shames neither, but to which each brings something personal.

The Song of Songs contains many clues to the mysteries and joys of sex. A reading of that book will show sometimes the woman taking the initiative and sometimes the man. All five senses come into play and there is spoken admiration of delight. It is natural to have a reticence over such matters, but within the privacy and purity of the marriage bed, it is important to remember that each one's pleasure is tied up with the pleasure of the other, and therefore it is an excellent and Scriptural idea to express delight.

7. SPENDING TIME

It sounds obvious but a relationship cannot prosper without an investment of time. Just because you live together doesn't mean you spend time together. There are the demands of work and church and children and wider family; there is the gym, the Irish wolfhound, and all that decking in the garden.

We loathe the expression 'quality time'; just time will do, time when you give your beloved your undivided attention, or time when you do together something that she likes, like football, or that he likes, like shopping. (No stereotypes here!) Or you could work on the decking together, or even better go to the prayer meeting together.

The Book of Proverbs tells us that a merry heart does good like a medicine. Sometimes we need that light touch. Time spent giggling over old photographs is not wasted time. Doing the tango in the kitchen will embarrass your children in front of their friends, but it is worth it.

A shared sense of humour is an intimate thing; single words, which have significance only to you, can occur in an unexpected context and lead to the sharing of a knowing smile. A repertoire of in-jokes, phrases or gestures strengthen the bond. At this point we should warn you about the man whose habit was to give his wife's suspenders a friendly twang through her skirt, when they were out walking side by side. The strange woman, whom he mistook for his wife, in Harrods did not appreciate it and there was an ugly scene! Even that story however went into the family mythology and was enjoyed freshly at every telling.

8. KEEPING PROMISES

This is truthfulness in action. Marriage is built on one big promise and it is a fitting expression of your commitment to that big promise if you keep the small ones, spoken and unspoken on a daily basis. In this deceitful world there is so much to let you down. You buy that face product which is supposed to reverse the effects of ageing and it doesn't deliver. Then again the future is shrouded in darkness: you can't count on it; in so many areas you don't know what will happen. But the faithful husband or wife as a fixed point in your life is a great source of confidence and assurance of stability. But only in as far as you are dependable.

This means that promises made like:

'I'll phone the man about the decking.'
'I'll collect Marigold from her trumpet lesson.'

– must be a fixed priority.

The unspoken promises are not less important. I read in the local newspaper about a couple who were celebrating their diamond wedding. The husband paid tribute to his wife thus: 'I've been married 60 years and we've never run out of toilet paper!' So the ironed shirt in the drawer, the rubbish taken out, the Irish Wolfhound exercised, the cup of tea in the morning – all these things are the little nails which support the structure of your marriage. It is worth noticing and celebrating them. See A for appreciation above.

9. SPEAKING TO GOD

Princess Diana famously complained that there were three in her marriage, by which she meant that the third party was an unwelcome intruder, who sabotaged any chance she had of enjoying married life.

But the Bible suggests that the best marriages have three in them:

A chord of three strands is not quickly broken (Ecclesiastes 4:12).

The third is, of course, no human agent, but God himself.

The apostle John challenges Christians to walk in the light, by which he means cultivate an honest and open relationship with God, who is light. As we do so, we draw closer to others who are similarly walking in the light (1 John 1:7).

Within marriage this is intimacy at the spiritual level. 1 Peter 3:7 describes married couples as heirs together of the gracious gift of life. You have both and equally received something precious, an inheritance which you can share in and explore and appreciate together. Times of prayer together should form an important, if necessarily short, part of your daily routine.

This is not always easy to achieve. Some people find praying out loud in front of someone else a problem. But they should take the risk and work at it and be encouraged to overcome their shyness and embarrassment. The reading of Scripture or singing of hymns together can help the tongue-tied to find the words to give expression to what they want and need to say to God. There are many resources and aids for family prayer times, but with or without them, the point is that if you are serious about your marriage such times must not be neglected.

Unless the Lord builds the house, the builders labour in vain (Psalm 127:1).

If you have read this far in this book and not thought that marriage is an awesome assignment, then we, the authors, have failed. You need help to live for God; you need help to build a marriage which will honour him. That subject on its own should fuel your prayers for a lifetime.

Chapter 5

When?

The Richard Curtis film of the nineties, *Four Weddings and a Funeral*, propagated (at least) four lies and one half-truth.

LIE NUMBER 1: Love is chiefly about sex.

LIE NUMBER 2: Marriage is chiefly about a wedding.

LIE NUMBER 3: Weddings are chiefly about fancy clothes, flowers, a ring and a cake.

LIE NUMBER 4: None of the above is of any lasting significance.

The HALF-TRUTH the film gave out loud and clear was that there is vast scope for unhappiness and dissatisfaction in any human relationship.

At the end of the film the central couple, played by Hugh Grant and Aimee Macdonald, stand in the rain and make the inane decision not to marry and yet still (by implication) commit to each other.

So, this chapter asks the question 'when should I get married?' and we will answer those four lies with truth and extend one half-truth with some Scriptural application.

LIE NUMBER 1: LOVE IS CHIEFLY ABOUT SEX
Of course, physical attributes are not irrelevant and mutual attraction is a key part of the plot in a relationship which leads to marriage. But in the best of relationships the delight in

the beloved's appearance follows rather than precedes a delight in the beloved's person. For example, my mother used to sing a popular ditty of the fifties which went:

> She's got eyes of blue. I never cared for eyes of blue!
> But she's got eyes of blue: that's my weakness now.

A more recent Richard Curtis romantic comedy, *Love Actually*, explored further the place of love in our lives by following a number of parallel 'love' stories. Among the most touching of these was the one about the actors who were making a pornographic film. The intended irony was that physical attraction between them was the least important aspect of their burgeoning friendship. What they really enjoyed was getting to know each other as people.

It follows that you should not marry until you know each other well and for most people that takes time, especially if you meet when you are young, when you are still developing your own outlook on life. So take it slowly.

Another good, if not fashionable, idea is to take advice. Ask a trusted friend if you think the one you have in mind is suited to you. Even better, ask your parents. Of course, parents can be biased or wrong, but they do have the advantage of probably knowing you better than anyone else does. You would be foolish not to at least give some serious consideration to their reasoning, should they advise against the match.

Most important of all for a Christian is that in the getting-to-know process, you should get to know each other before God. It might be helpful, before you marry, to know your intended's position on decking, extreme ironing, large household pets or trumpet playing, but it is not sufficient. You need to talk over the big questions like where you are going in life and what things are really important to you. You need to talk over what you are learning from Scripture; you need to begin to pray together.

Having stated a general agreement with the old proverb, 'marry in haste, repent at leisure', a caveat should be added. There is such a thing as too long an engagement, especially if the couple do not have the reasons of youth or financial dependence to hold them back. If the only reason for waiting is saving up to have the wedding of the century (and the Mother of all receptions), then see point 3 below and get on with it. One of the purposes for which God designed marriage is as a proper outlet for sexual expression. So, if a couple are mutually attracted (as they should be) and have declared their intentions by getting engaged, a long and purposeless engagement will put their respective self-control under a great deal of unnecessary pressure, especially in a climate where no one at the office will believe or understand their adherence to the principle of virginity and sexual purity.

In such a climate it is helpful to counter lie number one with the truth that love is about giving not having; it is about putting the welfare and happiness of the other above your own.

Lie Number 2: Marriage is Chiefly About a Wedding

The wedding is just one day, albeit a significant one, in your lives. Your marriage is about every day thereafter. The question 'when should I marry?' should include, therefore, careful consideration of what it will mean to live as a married person in the way that God intends married people to live, which is also, incidentally, the only way to be lastingly happy and married.

The potential bridegroom needs to be able to answer this question with a resounding 'negative':

'Apart from my faith in Jesus Christ, is there any thing I would not give up, if I knew it was for the good of my wife to do so?'

When he becomes a husband, a man becomes the head of his house. His job is to provide, protect and lead. Fulfilling such a job description will require sacrifice on his part, because always he will have in mind, not his own comfort and convenience, but the well-being of his wife. He will want her not just to survive but to flourish. You men, read again Ephesians 5:25-33, and dismiss any notions of tyrannical Victorian Papas.

The potential bride needs to be able to answer this question with a steady positive:

'If in the future my husband makes a decision, with which I do not agree, will I yet submit to and support him in that decision, provided that it does not impinge on my relationship with Jesus Christ?'

These are searching questions. It may be that in answering them, you discover that you are not ready to marry this person now or indeed at any time.

They are, however, questions of crucial importance. They expose the true depth of the love and trust you have in your intended spouse. Paul's last word on the subject of marriage in his letter to the Ephesians is that 'the wife must respect her husband'.

Too often, we have sat with miserable and beaten married couples whose story could be summed up in these two words: no respect.

Sometimes the lack of respect goes way back to before the wedding. Even in courtship, it was she who set the pace. She controlled everything about the wedding and honeymoon. Afterwards she controlled the finances and the child-rearing: she effectively gave him only a walk-on part in the play of their lives. And while she did all this because 'someone had to,' she bitterly resented it and him. It has led to the ruin of many a marriage.

He had initially been flattered by her attentions and had coalesced into all her plans. After all she was so much better at it than he was. She made sure he never got a chance to practise and in the end he believed her when she described him as weak and useless. He took the decision to retreat to his workshop, his office, an affair or even his decking.

We would plead with unmarried female readers of this book not to marry a man they cannot respect. We would plead with unmarried men to take courage and be men.

We would plead with married people who recognise a growing 'no respect' scenario emerging in their relationship, to repent and, with God's help, to change.

Marriage is about a commitment to live as man and woman, in the way that God prescribes in his word.

LIE NUMBER 3: WEDDINGS ARE CHIEFLY ABOUT FANCY CLOTHES, FLOWERS, A RING AND A CAKE

We are longing for the day when a Christian couple will be radical enough to get married in normal clothes, without the aid of huge floral arrangements, a towering white cake and (most of all) a photographer. Of course, we understand the desire to mark the day in some special way. It is a day of huge significance but the cultural trappings are not the significant thing about it.

What then is the significance of the wedding day? It is this: it marks an ending and a beginning, which is summed up in Genesis 2:24.

> For this reason a man will leave his father and mother and be united to his wife, and they will become one flesh.

The day you get married, you officially leave your parents' home, even if you have not resided there for some years. A whole new unit of society is established as you make your promises to your wife or husband. You leave your parents in more than a physical sense. A woman leaves the protection of her father and goes to the protection of her husband. That is what is behind the wholesome tradition of a young man asking the girl's father for permission to marry. It is signified in the wedding service by the question: 'Who gives this woman to be married to this man?'

There is for both parties a leaving in an emotional and psychological sense. No longer are your parents the first ones you run to share news or ask for help. They may still be the second ones, but the rule is, each other first. That is one of the implications of being united. You become a team and you express that, not by matching shirts, but by a matching outlook and direction and by a well-disciplined loyalty to each other.

So do not marry until you are ready to make that transfer.

LIE NUMBER 4: NONE OF THE ABOVE IS OF ANY LASTING SIGNIFICANCE

One of the great love songs of the sixties was Paul Simon's *Kathy's Song*.

My mind's distracted and confused,
My thoughts are many miles away,
They lie with you when you're asleep
And kiss you when you start your day.

In the seventies John Denver encountered huge success with his *Annie's Song*:

Come let me love you, let me always be
    with you.
Let me drown in your laughter, let me die
    in your arms.

The sad truth is that neither Paul's marriage to Kathy, nor John's to Annie, stood the test of time. They all ended up in the divorce court. Unbelievers will agree that it is sad and shake their heads muttering something about that being just the way it is and what can you do.

This book is written because there are some things you can do, the first of which is to recognise the true meaning of love and the truth about marriage.

Marriage is a solemn and binding covenant. Remember the words of Jesus:

So they are no longer two but one. Therefore what God has joined together, let man not separate (Matthew 19:6).

One of the implications of the lasting nature of marriage is that it is worth working at. The answer to the question, 'When can you stop working at your marriage?', is ' Not as long as you breathe.'

Perhaps John Denver and Paul Simon and the thousands of others whose marriages come to a sorry end every year have failed to understand the truth about marriage. Or even more likely they have not taken on board the wise advice encapsulated in Proverbs 14:23.

All hard work brings a profit,
But mere talk leads only to poverty.

Saying beautiful things is one thing, doing beautiful deeds is another. Reading a book on marriage and agreeing with every line is one thing, but you have to act upon it. It will sometimes be hard, painful work, because your failures will lead you to face up to some unpalatable truths about yourself, but it is profitable work You and your spouse will be better for it.

ONE HALF-TRUTH: THERE IS VAST SCOPE FOR UNHAPPINESS AND DISSATISFACTION IN RELATIONSHIPS Of course there is. Because of our rebellion against God, we engage in all manner of selfish and mean-spirited behaviours. Even Christians, indwelt by the Holy Spirit, yet grieve that same Spirit when they believe lies and make themselves the centre of their lives rather than God and his ways. When they do so they are frequently discouraged and justifiably depressed.

In the context of marriage, if things have gone sour, many become convinced that it can never be any different, that things can never change for the better. That too is a lie from the pit. When do you give up on your marriage? Answer: never! The Christian gospel is about change – there is always scope for hope and space for grace. God's word to the married person who is living selfishly or who is wrapped up in bitterness and resentment is the same as that to any sinner:

> Repent! Turn away from all your offences; then sin will not be your downfall. Rid yourselves of all the offences you have committed, and get a new heart and a new spirit. Why will you die O house of Israel? (Ezekiel 18:30, 31)

There is vast scope for unhappiness when we refuse to do things in God's way, continually laying the blame for the state of our marriage on the other party or on our circumstances. But the obsession of even post-modern secular culture with love, points to the fact that we are made in God's image for relationship with him and with others and that the deepest possible satisfaction and happiness are available in both those spheres.

Which way will you choose, for your life and your marriage? It is in one sense, a daily choice.

Chapter 6

Where?
The purpose of your marriage

A picturesque place of worship? A quaint chapel with roses in the garden? Your home church filled with smiling friends and relatives on a gorgeous sunny Spring day? Where a marriage takes place can be the stuff of dreams. And why not!

But we are not thinking here about the venue for your wedding ceremony. Though that might be an important consideration concerning the great day, it is not likely to be of much consequence for your marriage in the long term.

Let me ask you a rather different question. Where do you want your marriage to go? There all kinds of things to aim at in your life together. In which direction are you going to take your marriage? In other words, what do you see as the purpose of your marriage? What will you be trying to achieve through it?

As a bride and groom walk down the aisle, what agenda is at the back of their minds? It may be overstating it a bit, but is he thinking about her along these lines? 'You make me happy, and in getting married I'm giving *you* the opportunity to make *me* happy for the rest of your life.' She may be thinking something very similar about her own happiness as the purpose for which she got married.

As Christians we might feel a little uncomfortable about that. We can identify the selfishness in such attitudes. We might decide, therefore, that it is better to state the aim of marriage in terms of our happiness rather than my happiness. But the question is this: Is happiness, either individually or together, meant to be the purpose at the centre of your marriage? Is that meant to be where you aim to go together? I do not think it is.

One well-known Christian book on marriage, which has much good in it, tells us, with Genesis 2:24 in mind, that the purpose of marriage is 'oneness'. But I don't think that is true either. We have seen that oneness is indeed crucial to the 'what?' of marriage, but it does not give us the answer to the 'where?' Adam and Eve were at one in their decision to eat the forbidden fruit. But that did not mean they were using their marriage for the right purpose.

Other Christians might say that the target we should aim for in marriage is to serve one another. But though that is good and essential to a working marriage, I have to say that I do not think that is the main purpose either. A working engine is essential to a car, but having one does not guarantee you will drive it in the right direction. Many a car with a good engine has been driven over a cliff!

Of course God wants us to be happy in our marriages and at one in our marriages and to serve one another. But if we focus on these things there is a sense in which we are missing the wood for the trees. None of these things should be top of our marriage agenda. I have one simple message in this chapter that we need to get straight. It is of vital importance. Before all else, your marriage Christian, is for God. It is to carry through his agenda. That is the big picture which we must not miss. The direction of your marriage must be towards God and his glory and that direction must be explicit and consciously pursued. Where should your marriage be headed? It should be heading for God and his glory.

When there are serious problems in a Christian marriage, they are almost certainly first vertical before they are horizontal. Troubles in the relationship between a husband and wife more often than not, reflect problems in the relationship they have with God, either as individuals or as a couple. If the Lord is not at the centre of your personal lives and of your marriage, then simply improving communication skills or understanding gender differences better will not do. God and his glory must be your goal.

1. Prove it!
We can see this is true as we look at three great phases of redemption history – that is

from creation, salvation (new creation) and resurrection (new creation complete). We know this is true:

From Creation. Whatever else we may learn about marriage from the story of Adam and Eve, we must not forget they were God's creatures, living in God's world, under God's command, made in God's image, to carry out God's purposes. Their function was to carry out God's objective on earth (Genesis 1:26-28). Made in the image of God, they were created to obey him and represent him in the world. Yes, God gave them great freedom, e.g., Genesis 2:16, 17. But they were there for God, and so are we.

It was when, at the serpent's suggestion, Adam and Eve chose to listen to each other rather than to what God had said that things went disastrously wrong, for them as individuals, for their marriage, and for their children – the human race (Romans 5:15; I Corinthians 15:22). The warning is obvious, and we should take it seriously.

From Salvation. Let's ask the question, 'what is a Christian?' There are of course, many wonderful ways of giving an answer. A Christian is someone who is forgiven by God through his grace. A Christian is someone who has personal faith in the Lord Jesus Christ. A Christian is someone who is born of God's Holy Spirit. A Christian is a child of God. This encouraging list could go on and on.

But one definition is given by Paul in 2 Corinthians 5:15. The verse reads, 'And he died for all, that those who live should no longer live for themselves but for him who died for them and was raised again.' The 'he' Paul is speaking of, is of course, the Lord Jesus. But in this verse Paul gives another definition of a Christian. He tells us that Christians are people who no longer live life for themselves, but for the Lord who died for them. That living for the Lord is meant to be true in every area of our lives. And that includes marriage.

The Lord Jesus himself spells this out very bluntly. *If anyone comes to me and does not (by comparison) hate his father and mother, his wife and children, his brothers and sisters – yes, even his own life – he cannot be my disciple* (brackets mine) (Luke 14:26). Our marriage and family fall within the sphere over which Christ claims first place.

This may seem rather scary. We may think that Jesus is invading a space which somehow ought to be private and ours alone. But Christ will not in any way diminish your relationship. Rather he will enhance it. Just as the sun needs to be at the centre of our solar system so that its gravitational pull will hold everything together, so Christ needs to be at the centre of our marriages to stop them flying apart.

From Resurrection. The fact that our marriages are for God is also seen from the temporary nature of marriage. It is only for this life. Marriage is a great thing. But remember it is only a picture on earth of an even more wonderful marriage in heaven between God and his people. Do you remember Jesus' answer to the trick question from the Sadducees?

They posited the case of one woman who had consecutively had seven husbands. Whose wife would she be in the resurrection state? Jesus replied, *Are you not in error because you do not know the Scriptures or the power of God? When the dead rise, they will neither marry nor be given in marriage; they will be like the angels in heaven* (Mark 12:25). Marriage is only temporary. It is not an end in itself. It serves God's purposes.

There may be a tendency to be disappointed by the idea that marriage is a temporary arrangement. Many of us enjoy our marriages so much that we never want them to end. But that is to think the wrong way round. Rather we should understand that if the reality of which human marriage is only the picture is so great, how fantastic must be the reality of what God has in store for us in heaven in the marriage of Christ and his church. I am sure that nothing of what we treasure most about our marriages here will be missing in heaven. At the wedding, Jesus saved the best wine until last! (John 2:10)

The fact that our marriages have a limited time period also reminds us that though marriage is good we must not put unhelpful pressure on single people to get hitched. I saw a quote recently from a single guy about how he stopped people bugging him all the time about getting married. He said, 'Old aunts used to come up to me at weddings, poking me in the ribs and gleefully whispering, "you're next."' 'They stopped,' he said, 'when I started doing the same to them at funerals.'

According to I Corinthians 7 single people can serve God well. Our marriages are meant to serve God too. Where is your marriage going to go?

2. Apply it!

When God is removed as the ruler of our hearts, as the agenda setter in the marriage, it is bound to lead to trouble of one sort or another.

Is the highest commitment in your marriage going to be to your own personal happiness?

- Will the root of the trouble between you be, that you are angry that your mate has not delivered what you expected for your pleasure? Jesus parable of the tree and its fruit tells us that our actions reveal our hearts, (Luke 6:43-45). The things we do in our marriages also reveal our hearts.
- Will the greatest priority each year be to make sure that you are able to book a luxury holiday which will be the envy of your friends? There is nothing wrong with having a holiday, but should it have such a high priority? And aren't there a lot of Christian summer outreaches which need supporting?
- Will the highest commitment in your marriage be to your mutual satisfaction rather than to the Lord and his glory? Or will the focus be on what is best for your children? Will it be, for example, to do with making sure they get to the best possible school? If so, I have to tell you that you will be going in the wrong direction. Important though your children indeed are, they are not more important than God.
- Will you be blaming your partner for the problems in your marriage when in fact

the problem is in your heart relationship to God? A lip service to following Christ, while the heart is enslaved to materialism and prosperity is often a problem here. Jesus warned us that *you cannot serve both God and money* (Matthew 7:24). Sadly, there are many who call themselves Christians, whose main priority is not serving the gospel but rather making sure they live in a 'nice' area. Don't set your heart on such things. It may well lead to trouble between you. An idol will have intruded in the place of God.

It is always easier to see our marriage partner's faults than our own (Matthew 7:3-5). God calls us to peace. He has clearly described to us in his Word how a husband and wife should relate together. There may be times when we need to stop blaming each other for problems between us in a marriage and humbly admit that wrong objectives have been ruling your hearts? God wants us to repent of our idols and make Jesus Lord of our marriages. Idols always disappoint and dehumanize us (Psalm 115:4-8). Where is your marriage going? Let the Lord set the agenda? Let the Lord give you directions as to where to go.

As we do that, I can assure you there will

be blessing for both partners and the whole family. At a recent London Men's Convention, David Jackman was asked what one piece of advice he would give to newly married people. His answer was immediate. *Seek first God's kingdom and his righteousness...* (Matthew 6:33).

Appendix 1

Pre-marriage Studies

Preparing for Marriage

Most churches are happy to provide a simple course for those who are about to get married. Here we include two short studies which might be used as the basis for marriage preparation classes. We recommend that the church asks a married couple who are mature Christians with a good marriage to act as mentors for these studies for those contemplating marriage. The engaged couple should first of all complete a study together, then bring their answers to a meeting for discussion of their answers with their mentors. It should be underlined that the major benefit of these studies will come from the private discussions between the engaged couple on the issues raised. There are two separate studies and it is best that there are two separate meetings with the mentors. If the mentoring couple could invite the engaged couple to their house and engage with them in discussion over a pleasant meal that would be all the better. The studies should be carried out sometime in the 6 months running up to the wedding, but not too close to the wedding day, to allow a bit of breathing space before it happens.

Study 1

Study the following questions and discuss them together writing your answers in a notebook. Bring your questions and answers with you when you meet with your pre-marriage mentors. Spend the time talking through your answers with them..

A. GOD'S DESIGN FOR MARRIAGE
Read Genesis 2:18-25

1. Who originated the idea of marriage?

2. Give at least four purposes which marriage was intended to fulfill (see also Genesis 1:28 and Ephesians 5:22-33).

3. What do the words 'suitable helper' (Genesis 2:18) imply about the man? What do they imply about the role of the woman?

4. According to Genesis 2:24, which human relationship in life takes precedence over all others?

5. What, in practice, does leaving father and mother mean for the newly married couple?

6. What do the words 'they will become one flesh' signify?

7. List some things that married people ought to do to promote and display this oneness.

B. The Wife's Responsibility
Read Ephesians 5:22-23

1. What is the one word that summarizes the wife's first responsibility to her husband? (see also 1 Peter 3:1).

2. What do the words 'as to the Lord' (v. 22) suggest about the wife's submission?

3. According to verse 24, how extensive should a wife's submission be?

4. What limit is put on the wife's submission by Colossians 3:18 and Acts 5:29?

5. According to verse 33, what should the woman's attitude be to her husband? What does this mean in practice? How do you think this helps the husband?

C. The Husband's Responsibility
Read Ephesians 5:22-33

1. What two words in the passage summarize the husband's responsibility to his wife? Compare verse 23 and verse 25.

2. What example or model must the husband keep constantly in mind as he exercises headship in the family?

3. For whose benefit is the headship of Christ always exercised? Compare Ephesians 1:22 and 5:25-27. For whose benefit, therefore, should

the headship of the husband be exercised?

4. Consider the ways in which Christ loved the church and brings her to fulfilment and 'radiance' and apply them to the way a husband should love his wife.

5. How does a right exercise of headship and love by the husband make the wife feel about her submission?

D. COMMUNICATION

1. Oneness in marriage cannot come about without good communication between the couple. Look at Ephesians 4:15 and write down the two key words fundamental to good communication.

2. Four very obvious things must happen between the two of you in order for there to be meaningful dialogue. One person must speak; the second person must listen; the second person must speak; the first person must listen. According to James 1:19 what do most of us need to learn about carrying out a helpful conversation?

3. List some ways in which people can communicate without words. How will you use eyes and hands both to enhance communication and to signal that this is a time for serious listening and talking?

4. Read the following list of levels of communication:

casual conversation/ saying things which are encouraging and supportive/ talking in clichés/ planning or decision making/ making your needs known/ sharing facts/ sharing ideas and opinions/ speaking and receiving words of correction/ sharing feelings and emotions.

Rewrite the list in order of intimacy i.e. from 1. the most superficial down to 9. the most intimate. Circle those at which you think you as a couple have greatest difficulty in communicating.

5. Discuss the importance of Proverbs 18:2, Proverbs 18:13 and Matthew 7:1-5 to good communication.

6. Read the list of the fruit of the Holy Spirit in Galatians 5:22-23. Comment on how each of these will be shown in your speaking and listening.

E. FORGIVENESS

1. See Matthew 5:23,24 and 1 Peter 3:7. What do these verses teach about the connection between human relationships and your relationship with God?

2. When you know you're in the wrong. See Luke 15:11-24. What can we learn from the prodigal son about how to seek forgiveness?

3. When you believe you've been wronged. What does Matthew 18:21-35 teach you about why you should grant forgiveness, and how to do it?

4. According to 1 Peter 3:7, what will be a good sign that any troubles between you have been sorted out?

Study 2

Whereas the first study was centred on Biblical principles this second study encourages you to consider how those principles apply to you as specific people as you get married.

Study the following questions and discuss them together writing your answers in a notebook. Bring your questions and answers with you when you meet with your pre-marriage mentors. Spend the time talking through your answers with them.

A. SOME AIMS FOR YOUR MARRIAGE

Before we set out on anything in life it is good to ask ourselves what we are seeking to achieve. What are some worthwhile aims which *you* hope to achieve together through your marriage ?

B. KNOW YOURSELVES

I. Imagine you are each bringing to your marriage a suitcase with all your background, upbringing and past experiences packed inside. Unpack to each other the three most important items in your suitcases.

2. Celebrate the differences between you. Each of you make a list of the attributes (positive and negative) of the other. Then compare the lists.

3. When do strengths become weaknesses? For example, you might be a very well informed person who is able to talk freely on current affairs. But this strength, if not controlled, could turn you into an argumentative bore. Honestly consider your strengths and identify in what ways they could become a weakness and a source of irritation to your partner.

4. Read I Corinthians 13:4-7. Consider the way in which love behaves: each of you choose three of the elements Paul lists and, bearing in mind your future partner's personality or circumstances, complete a sentence for each element describing how you intend to be a loving wife/husband to him/her. Make it specific to your relationship, e.g. *love is patient:* 'I will love my wife by making only supportive comments when she has to work inconvenient hours.'

C. ACHIEVING ONENESS IN THE WAY YOU LIVE

Given the fact that we all tend to think that our own life patterns are the most reasonable and justifiable, it is important that certain issues are discussed and helpful habits agreed and established at the outset of your married life.

Keeping in mind the aims you have set for your marriage and the principles of *headship, love* and *submission* we looked at in Study 1, how will you divide or share responsibilities? What are the potential pitfalls and what will your priorities be with regard to the following issues?

a) socialising with friends
b) your jobs/careers
c) planning a family
d) housework
e) money
f) meal preparation
g) family prayers
h) church life
i) relating to parents
j) leisure activities

D. About Sex
*Read 1 Corinthians 7:2-5, 9
and Proverbs 5:15-21*

a) *The purposes of sex*

1. From the above Bible passages and also Genesis 1:27, 28 and Genesis 2:18,24, list the purposes of sex in marriage. You should find at least four.

2. Why is sex outside of marriage wrong?

b) *The purity of sex in marriage*

1. What does Hebrews 13:4 say about sex within marriage?

2. What does Matthew 5: 27, 28 teach about keeping your marriage pure?

c) *The pleasure of sex in marriage*

1. What does Proverbs 5:19 teach about enjoying sex within marriage?

2. What attitude towards the marriage partner and his/her body are encouraged by Song of Solomon 4:1-7 and 5:10-16?

d) *The planning of a family*

1. Read Genesis 1:28 and Psalm 127:3, 4. How should a Christian view the arrival of children?

2. What Biblical principles are there to guide you in planning your family? See 1 Timothy 5:8 and Philippians 2:4.

3. There are two methods of birth control which Scripture forbids. Find them by referring to Exodus 20:13 and 1 Corinthians 7:5.

E. AN ENDURING MARRIAGE
Read Matthew 5:31, 32 and Matthew 19:1-9

1. How long is marriage supposed to last ?
2. Read Malachi 2:13-16. What does God

hate? Where are we to guard our marriages first of all ?

3. List some implications which emerge from the fact that marriage is a permanent relationship.

If you have any questions which occur to you which are not covered in these studies, make a note of them and talk them through with your mentors. They may be able to help you. It is helpful that you talk through whatever is important to you.

Appendix 2

Why not?
Sexual temptation
in the workplace

Why not?
Sexual temptation in the workplace

Before people get married there are questions which they need to face. God wants us to think those issues through seriously. But once we are married it will not be long for most people before the devil comes along with a question. The devil's question will have to do with breaking your marriage vows. He will tempt you to destroy that oneness which is at the heart of marriage and can speak so eloquently of the wonderful love between Christ and the church. 'Commit adultery?' The devil will ask, 'why not?'

We have to be realistic about the world we live in. Though as we contemplate marriage we might say to ourselves that we would never do such a thing and that a broken marriage would never happen to us, the statistics are that something like 30% to 40% of marriages end in divorce. Do we think that somehow temptation will always pass us by? Is the devil really that kind? Rather, with stark realism the Bible tells us all, 'if you think you are standing firm, be careful that you don't fall' (1 Corinthians 10:12). There is no room for complacency.

As a working pastor and wife we have had the sad duty from time to time of trying to re-forge marriages that are falling apart. Thankfully, this situation does not come around very often. But having sat and listened to the tragic tales of how a husband or wife has gone astray and started becoming involved with someone else, we have found that very often it is the workplace where the illicit relationship began. It is through someone at the office, or the college or wherever we earn our wages, that Satan has had the opportunity to whisper 'Why not?' Of course, it can happen anywhere. But with so many wives and husbands working these days and spending a great deal of time with other people at their place of employment, quite frequently this is where the problems arise. So it is worth thinking carefully about the subject of sexual temptation in the workplace.

One of the most famous attempted seduction stories in the Bible is that of young Joseph being tempted by Potiphar's wife. At this point in his life, Joseph was not married. But she was. And it is noteworthy that the tale of Joseph's battle with sexual temptation in Genesis 39, occurred in his place of work. He was a slave to one of Pharaoh's officials. What can we learn from the attempted seduction in Potiphar's house?

A Place of Danger

Why can the workplace be a dangerous place sexually? Aside from the fact that these days people of both genders generally go out to work, there are a number of reasons why our place of employment might present a temptation.

Atmosphere. Joseph (v. 1), had been taken from the Promised Land to Egypt. He had been taken from a place where God was known and his righteous requirements acknowledged, to a place where they were not. Sadly, it is frequently like that for many Christians as they travel from home to work. Home is where we pray and read our Bibles. But most offices, factories, colleges and shops know nothing of God these days. You enter an amoral environment, where pragmatism and profit are the only rules. The idea of Bible ethics in business is frequently not only despised but seen as a positive impediment to progress. An amoral atmosphere in business ethics can easily spill over into personal ethics and that can lower our defences. 'No one cares here, so why not?'

Time. Joseph was spending a lot of time around Potiphar's wife (v. 2). We spend around a third of our week with our colleagues at work. When you take into account long hours of work, the time spent commuting, sleep and time with the children you may be more often alone with colleagues than you are with your wife or husband. On top of that, people in similar situations, under similar pressures, spending lots of time together do develop a closeness. At one level there is nothing wrong with that. It is good when there is a team-spirit in the company, among colleagues. But if that closeness is with a colleague of the opposite sex, it may get too close.

Stress. It would be no surprise if Joseph felt pretty vulnerable at this time. After all, he had just been rejected by his family and had suffered the indignity of being sold as a slave. Here he was in a foreign land where no one knew or cared about him. Confused and hurting he may well have felt the need for some affection and tenderness.

Despite their controlled exterior, the workplace is a place where people often get hurt emotionally. Targets are not met and the boss gives you a hard time. You miss out on that promotion. You have a bad day and are made to look dumb by someone who is your junior. The competition and stress of the business world can leave people lonely, tired and feeling vulnerable. And that is just the time where we might long for consolation from 'someone who understands.' Except that someone might be another colleague rather than your spouse. He or she is right there, just after you have come out of being carpeted by the CEO. Your wife or your husband is miles away. 'Why not cry on that colleague's shoulder? She has always been so kind to you. Why not?' The first steps to adultery have often been along such a path.

Authority. With the current awareness of sexual harassment in our culture, perhaps this is not the problem it once was. But here we find Joseph being asked for sexual favours by a superior, his boss's wife. She was someone who could put in a good word for him and see him promoted or could get him sacked (v. 7, v. 10, v. 11). The workplace always has a power structure that can be misused to bring sexual pressure to bear.

These factors are worth contemplation. Perhaps the relationships in your office or warehouse or travel agency or wherever you work are good and right. But do not be naive. A husband and wife need to talk these kinds of issues through.

TAKING STEPS

What can we do to protect ourselves from sexual temptation at work? Some ideas present themselves from the story of Joseph.

Be an up-front Christian. Even though Joseph was a slave he witnessed to his faith in God, verse 9. That did not put off Potiphar's wife, but it might put off some people from making advances. Why not have a Bible or New Testament on your desk at work. It could act as a reminder to you of your commitment to Christ, and act as a friendly signal to others of where you stand.

Be walking with God. The recurring theme in Genesis 39 is 'the LORD was with Joseph' (vv. 2, 3, 5, 21). It was because God was with Joseph that Joseph had the strength and the sense to resist the seduction when it came. We need to maintain the spiritual basics of prayer, worship, Bible reading, witness, fellowship and honesty. It is worth remembering that before James tells us to, 'Resist the devil,' he emphasizes the need to, 'Submit yourselves then, to God' (James 4:7). If God is with us and we are with God the devil flees.

Be up-front about your marriage. It helps if, without becoming boring, you mention your marriage partner in conversation at work from time to time. Never ever speak about your spouse disparagingly to other people. That will only give a green light to those who may wish to trap you sexually. Instead, speak well of your marriage and your marriage partner. This will send out a positive, 'leave me alone' signal to others. Reading Joseph's story, the great thing about him was his openness and honesty at all times. It is good, if a wife and husband who are working, talk together often about work, the people at work and what's going on there. Do not keep each other in the dark. Let one another ask whatever questions occur. Be transparent with your spouse about work. And when it comes to the company's sports day, or the office party, take your wife or husband with you.

Beware of rationalisations. Falling into immorality or adultery always involves a process. It does not just happen out of the blue.

Step 1 takes place in the thoughts.

Step 2 involves some positive signal from the object of desire.

Step 3 involves the emotional attachment nurtured by both people.

Step 4 is finding the time and place.

Step 5 is the sin.

At each point down that deadly path our sinful nature will find an excuse, for you to go ahead to the next step. 'It is only a thought, it can't do any harm.' 'We are close, but we are doing nothing wrong.' 'Everyone is allowed one mistake.' Give no room to such rationalisations. Joseph gets 'the come on' loud and clear, but he will not allow sin a foothold, even in his mind. 'How then could I do such a wicked thing and sin against God?' (v. 9).

Be ready to run. In the end, the pressure was such that Joseph had to simply take to his heels (v. 12). Perhaps someone reading this finds themselves getting involved too deeply with someone in their place of work. It is better to run, to resign your job, than to wreck your spiritual life and if you have one, your family. To run may initially bring trouble, but it will eventually bring blessing, even as it did for Joseph.

Lastly, as there are people married or contemplating marriage reading this, perhaps I ought to address you as the other partner. Be aware that when your spouse goes to work he or she may enter a world with its own peculiar set of sexual temptations. You, do your best to make sure that home is the best place and that the relationship with you is the source of tenderness and joy that it ought to be (Proverbs 5:18, 19).

Other books
of interest
from
Christian Focus

aren't they lovely when they're asleep?

Lessons in unsentimental parenting

ann benton

Aren't they lovely when they're asleep?

Lessons in unsentimental parenting
Ann Benton

Ann Benton used to run parenting skills classes in local schools. People kept saying "This is great, where do you get this stuff?" She came clean "Actually, it's from the Bible."

This book contains the wisdom distilled from Ann's popular seminars on parenting the next generation. She uses a 'God's eye view' of what we are really like in order to help people who are seeking to be responsible parents in an increasingly child-centred society.

You will learn six key concepts: accept, beware, communicate, discipline, evaluate and fear the Lord. These are applied with understanding and sensitivity.

At last – a parenting book with authority and easy to understand applications! Each short, punchy chapter is rounded off with thought-provoking questions that will make you want to wake them up and try some new ideas!

ISBN 1-85792-876-8

....of Such is the Kingdom

Nurturing Children in the Light of Scripture

Timothy A. Sisemore

Are you, and your church, bringing up children the way God wants you to?

Sisemore teaches you about - Christian parenting in a hostile world, educating children spiritually and academically, disciplining and discipling, honouring parents, how are children saved?, The church's responsibility towards its children.

'Anyone who has a true concern for the spiritual welfare of children in this present age must read this book!'

Mark Johnston,
Pastor and Conference speaker

'Here is a straightforward, readable, challenging and practical manual - just what parents are looking for.'

Sinclair B. Ferguson,
Professor of Systematic Theology

Timothy A. Sisemore is Professor of Counseling at the Psychological Studies Institute in Atlanta and Chattanooga. He is married to Ruth and they have one daughter, Erin.

ISBN 1-85792-514-9

The Family you Want

How to Establish an Authentic, Loving home

John A. Huffman

Whilst we all have a deep longing to be part of an ideal family, imperfect people make imperfect ones – it's a simple fact of life. Should we, as some in our post-modern society suggest, just give up?

If that thought depresses you then take heart and let John Huffman help you to achieve the best family you can. It won't be perfect but it will be better.

'I highly recommend it… His approach is thoughtful, his style clear… this book is authentic.'

Leighton Ford

"here is healing medicine for all who care about the family"

Harold Myra, Christianity Today

John Huffman has counselled many on family life issues and lectured internationally on the subject. He is the senior minister of St. Andrews Presbyterian Church in Newport Beach, California

ISBN 1-85792-933-0

WOMANHOOD
REVISITED

A FRESH LOOK AT THE ROLE OF WOMEN IN SOCIETY

ANNE GRAHAM

Womanhood Revisited

A Fresh look at the Role of Women in Society

Anne Graham

Why do so many full-time mothers and home-makers feel inferior to career women? Why do women feel they need to be more like men to be seen to be successful?

In her book Anne Graham suggests it is time to revisit the perfection of creation where woman was created for and from man – equal in value yet different in purpose, to live in co-operation and not competition.

'Anne has brought the roles of men and women under severe scrutiny as she examines the Word of God. Society, fashions and technology may change and advance, but God's Word remains relevant. Anne's efforts have been well worthwhile and will be a challenge and encouragement to all who read it.'

Fiona Castle, Author

Anne Graham trained as a doctor but has spent most of her energy as a wife to Jim, a Baptist minister, mother to four children and grandmother to 8. She is a popular speaker on this subject at home and abroad.

ISBN I-85792-685-4

Christian Focus Publications

publishes books for all ages

Our mission statement –

STAYING FAITHFUL

In dependence upon God we seek to help make his infallible word, the Bible, relevant. Our aim is to ensure that the Lord Jesus Christ is presented as the only hope to obtain forgiveness of sin, live a useful life and look forward to heaven with him.

REACHING OUT

Christ's last command requires us to reach out to our world with his gospel. We seek to help fulfill that by publishing books that point people towards Jesus and for them to develop a Christ-like maturity. We aim to equip all levels of readers for life, work ministry and mission.

Books in our adult range are published in three imprints.

Christian Heritage contains classic writings from the past.
Mentor focuses on books written at a level suitable for Bible College and seminary students, pastors, and other serious readers; the imprint includes commentaries, doctrinal studies, examination of current issues, and church history.
Christian Focus contains popular works including biographies, commentaries, basic doctrine, and Christian living. Our children's books are also published in this imprint.

Christian Focus Publications, Ltd
Geanies House, Fearn, Ross-shire,
IV20 1TW, Scotland, United Kingdom
info@christianfocus.com

For details of our titles visit us on our website
www.christianfocus.com